YOUR KNOWLEDGE HAS VALUE

Yasir Farabi

Why is leadership important for delivering successful projects? Leadership theories, methods and concepts

GRIN Verlag

Bibliografische Information der Deutschen Nationalbibliothek:

Die Deutsche Bibliothek verzeichnet diese Publikation in der Deutschen National-
bibliografie; detaillierte bibliografische Daten sind im Internet über http://dnb.d-
nb.de/ abrufbar.

Imprint:

Copyright © 2012 GRIN Verlag GmbH
Druck und Bindung: Books on Demand GmbH, Norderstedt Germany
ISBN: 978-3-656-25950-3

This book at GRIN:

http://www.grin.com/en/e-book/197076/why-is-leadership-important-for-delivering-
successful-projects-leadership

GRIN - Your knowledge has value

Der GRIN Verlag publiziert seit 1998 wissenschaftliche Arbeiten von Studenten, Hochschullehrern und anderen Akademikern als eBook und gedrucktes Buch. Die Verlagswebsite www.grin.com ist die ideale Plattform zur Veröffentlichung von Hausarbeiten, Abschlussarbeiten, wissenschaftlichen Aufsätzen, Dissertationen und Fachbüchern.

Visit us on the internet:

http://www.grin.com/

http://www.facebook.com/grincom

http://www.twitter.com/grin_com

IN WHAT KEY WAYS IS LEADERSHIP IMPORTANT TO DELIVERING SUCCESSFUL PROJECTS? WHAT LEADERSHIP METHODS, THEORIES AND/OR CONCEPTS ARE MOST HELPFUL IN UNDERSTANDING EFFECTIVE PROJECT LEADERSHIP AND WHY?

Introduction

Leadership has long been considered as an essential success factor in business, government, and military environments. However, the optimal style of leadership in a particular organizational setting still remains unclear. Increasing public scrutiny of leaders has also raised the question of what leadership style is to be put in action that can guarantee success. Therefore, the purpose of this report is to identify and analyse in what key ways leadership is important to delivering successful projects and also what leadership theories, methods and concepts are most helpful in understanding effective project leadership. With a view to achieving these objectives, this report at first spots some key factors of effective leadership and then discusses few concepts that are momentous in delivering present day views of leadership.

The periphery of such undertaking is enormous and it is quite complex to capture an instant snap shot across a number of leadership strategies. In order to react to the changing global environment, leaders consistently modify their strategies and behaviours. Therefore, the paper has attempted to limit the depth of investigation across the various measurement criteria because of time and resource constraints. Nonetheless, these can be satisfactorily used for high level evaluation.

Importance of leadership in delivering successful projects

Leadership, being different from management, requires different knowledge; different skill set and accomplishes different purpose. While management deals with the present, the resources and the facts; leadership deals with the future, the people and personalities and the ideas.

The first rule of effective leadership is to identify and maintain awareness of critical success factors. Things that matter most should not be left at the mercy of things that matter least. As aptly put by Ingen (2007, p. 55), a project leader must characterize the project drivers. A clear focus on priority prevents the project from being distracted. Setting and actively monitoring the goals is also crucial in delivering success because without knowing the destination, a project may end up at someplace undesirable. To establish team goals, leader presents a set of project goals at the kick-off meetings and team progress is to be reviewed against these goals, celebrating success and capturing lessons learned from the failures. Leader has to create an environment for success. Leader provides a clear vision on what success looks like and how it can be achieved. A successful leader lays a firm foundation with the bricks that others have thrown at him. Developing a comprehensive execution plan is the key to turn lemons into lemonade. Understanding the power environment of the organization and the position of its actors is also vital to the success of a project (Lovell, 1993, p. 76). As identified by Block (1983, p. 198), this understanding is a combination of conscious and intuitive, almost instinctive, thought process leading to actions. Failure to understand and control the political process has been the cause of downfall of many projects (Heery, 1998, p. 255). Block (1983, p. 2000) identified that successful project leader has to understand the organization's formal structure, its informal structure such as friendships, alliances; and also its environment such as each player's motivation, priorities and values.

A successful leader is responsible for clear communication. A vast majority of project failures can be traced, directly or indirectly, to communication failures (Ingen, 2007, p. 57). The number of communication channels increase exponentially with the size of project team. Regular project updates and formal presentations and communications to defined stakeholders and frequent governance meetings are formal means, while the informal ones require more face ensuring currency in knowledge and not to mention tapping into the grapevine (Bourne, 2008, p. 16). Moreover, Briner, Hastings and Geddes (1996, p. 155) are of the opinion that maintenance in the form of active communication also provides early warnings. Durable relationship is the key to surviving and thriving in the organizational political structure through peaceful settlement of differences (Briner et al., 1996, p. 72). The person who does the most talking and a successful leader are rarely the same person. There is a time to talk and there is a time to listen and a good leader allocates attention properly. Since team members were hired because of their expertise, actively listening to them breeds respect, trust and confidence because at the end of the day people will forget what someone said, people will forget what someone did, but they will never forget what someone made them feel (Ingen, 2007, p. 56).

An effective leader does not think himself as a new way of acting; rather he acts himself into a new way of thinking. Bourne (2008, p. 15) finds a very few leader that are good at anticipating, identifying and knowing how to dilute disasters caused by equivocal power relationships. According to Briner et al. (1996, p. 76), every organization has its own dynamics, distinctive pattern of actions and reaction to which an effective leader can read and adapt to. It is imperative for a project leader to understand how to react in a particular situation and if necessary, adapt behaviours to ensure success. According to Thompson (2011, p. 32), the emphasis must be on striking a balance between deliberate rational thoughtful strategies as well as supporting the psychology of emotive and intuitive aspects. Leader must also be able to recognize the danger signals, the early warning system, the warning of possible conflict with any stakeholder group. As mentioned by Boddy and Buchanan (1992, p. 254), only a project leader who has built credibility and knows how to tap into the power structures can defuse potential crisis. The main leadership skills still around are: being able to evaluate the effect and urgency of the issue and provide options and recommendations accordingly (Bourne, 2008, p. 17). As aptly put by Block (1983, p. 186), anticipating problems and planning long term strategies in a well thought-out manner can eventually lead to good solutions.

Implementation of a project often involves unexpected and unpredictable changes because it is a dynamic process. Therefore, a successful leader does not only provide momentum to the team effort but also is flexible in allowing changes by becoming a change agent. A leader should be able to anticipate and manage both external and internal changes all the time to become successful in today's ever changing global business environment. According to Yu (2006, p. 13), for external changes, the leader should possess the abilities to observe the situation sensibly, fathom the facts and adversities which emerge during the course of the project and foresee the coming changes and their impacts. In order to response to agile and competitive external environment, leaders should be able to create and change internal strategies from time to time which may include changes in resource planning and actions in order to better adapt to the changes maintaining high competitiveness and efficiency (Yu, 2006, p. 13). Team members or followers, who are not well adapted to the change or may be resistant to the change, can be persistently driven by telling and selling strategy. Changes not only bring in challenges but also opportunities. Apart from leadership to drive the right strategies for the change, it also indispensably needs management to manipulate resources, control actions and move the team forward incrementally toward the destination they envisioned.

Leadership Theories, Methods & Concepts

The study of leadership theory has been of the interest to the researchers since the time of Confucius in 5000 B.C. (Levine, 2000, p. 13). The importance of leadership in group endeavours has led to the development of a range of theories pertaining to leadership.

Some of the earliest leadership theories were based on Great Man theory (Carlyle, 1841; Dowd, 1936; Galton, 1870; Wiggam, 1931; Woods, 1913). The idea behind the theory is that leaders are different from their followers for their superior qualities genetically bestowed upon them. The search for these qualities or traits has led to the Trait theory of leadership, which views leadership as an assortment of characteristics that could be measured and distinguished from non-leaders (Gray & Smeltzer, 1989). However, the interest on Trait theory has eventually wither away as Stogdill (1948) has found Trait theory grounded upon weak and inconclusive study. Another group of early theorists have identified time, place and circumstance to be the cause of emergence of a leader, which became known as Environmental theory (Bogardus, 1918; Hocking, 1924; Mumford, 1909; Tead, 1935). Personal-situational theorists further expanded upon the Environmental theory by ascertaining interaction between the leader and followers as well as interaction between the leader and the environment (Case, 1933; Cattell, 1951; Gerth & Mills, 1952; Stogdill & Shartle, 1955; Westburgh, 1931). The Situational Leadership model (Hersey & Blanchard, 1977) is a more recent application of this theory, which describes that depending on different situational variables, leaders choose the best course of action. Therefore, it may be contended that not all style of leadership is appropriate for certain types of decision making. Another expansion of the test of leadership in combination with situation, and personal interactions is introduced by the Interaction-Expectation theory, which describes that leadership efficiency increases with the increase in the frequency of interaction between leader and followers (Evans, 1970; Fiedler, 1967; Hemphill, 1954; Homans, 1950).

During the 1970's, a majority of the researches began to emphasize, first, on transactional leadership theory, and later transformational leadership theory (Levine, 2000, p. 15). Transactional theory views leadership as an exchange between leaders and followers (Burns, 1978), while Transformational theory extended it to develop a unit of measurement for transformational leadership (Bass, 1985). A transactional leader has the power to perform certain tasks and the authority to reward or punish for team performance (Burns, 1978). This allows the leader to manage his group and the group agrees to follow his lead in exchange for reward. Leader corrects and trains his followers when productivity is sub-par and rewards effectiveness when expected goal is achieved. Transformational leadership, on the other hand, makes the group focused on the desired outcome through effective communication and motivates its group to be effective and efficient (Burns, 1978). A transformational leader focuses on the big picture and requires people to take care of minor details. Leader of this trait is highly visible and uses a chain of command to get the job done. Bass developed a model of six measurable variables that contribute to a full-range leadership style. Transformational leaders enthuse and encourage followers to go beyond their perceived abilities. Whether these leaders exist and whether they contribute positively is the topic for present day's research (Levine, 2000, p. 16).

With a view to addressing specific leader behaviours expected to contribute to organizational effectiveness, Functional leadership theory emerged (Hackman & Walton, 1986; McGrath, 1962), which explains that a leader's prime task is to take care of whatever his group needs to function effectively and cohesively (Fleishman et al., 1991; Hackman & Wageman, 2005; Hackman & Walton, 1986). To facilitate these functions a variety of leadership behaviours are expected. Fleishman (1953) identified that subordinates perceived their supervisors' behaviour in terms of two broad categories: consideration and initiating structure. While consideration includes behaviour involved in fostering effective relationships, initiating structure involves the actions of the leader focused specifically on task accomplishment. Although this theory is often applied to team leadership (Zaccaro, Rittman, & Marks, 2001), it may be applied to organizational leadership as well (Zaccaro, 2007).

This could include role clarification, setting performance standards, and holding subordinates accountable to those standards. Very recently another leadership theory emerged from Oxford School of Leadership, which states that leadership is created through the materialization of information by the leader or other stakeholders, not through the true actions of the leader himself (Adair, 1997). According to the view of Brobbey et al. (2009, p. 25) modern society media report their own views of a leader, which may be based on reality, but may also be based on a political command, a payment, or an inherent interest of the author, media, or leader. Therefore, it can be contended that the perception of a leader is created and in fact, may not reflect true leadership qualities at all.

Conclusion

The report asserts leadership as the process of exercising the influence between a leader and followers that is necessary to attain project's goals. Successful leaders empower, envision, energize and inspire people to achieve success. Today's project leader should blend management and leadership roles in conducting a project and learn to master both leadership and management skills to achieve success through the supports and actions from the team. Project leadership and management should juxtapose symbiotically in the teamwork in the process of a project.

Leadership can be learned and developed through on-job training and personal life experience. An effective leader should be passionate about his duty and work, set out the vision and objectives and share the vision with the followers, he or she should also be persistent in achieving the prescribed vision and objectives, embrace changes in strategy and direction during the course of project implementation; he or she should strike a good balance in using directive and supportive behaviours in the process of team development. More importantly a leader should take full responsibility when things do not go right, but behave in a self-effacing and understated manner and be prepared to attribute success to factors other than their own leadership.

References

Adair, J. (1997). *Decision Making and Problem Solving Strategies*. New York: Kogan Page Publishers.

Bass, B.M. (1985). *Leadership and performance beyond expectations*. New York: Free Press.

Block, R. (1983). *The Politics of Projects*. New Jersey, USA: Yourdon Press.

Boddy, D. & Buchanan, D. (1992). *Take the Lead: Interpersonal Skills for Project Managers*. New York, USA: Prentice Hall.

Bogardus, E.S. (1918). *Essentials of social psychology*. Los Angeles: University of Southern California Press.

Bourne, L. (2008). What Does a Project Manager Need to Deliver Successful Projects. *Project Management Leadership*, 4(1), 1-22.

Briner, W., Hastings, C. & Geddes, M. (1996). *Project Leadership*. Aldershot, Hampshire: Gower Publications.

Brobbey, C., Puplampu, R., Adjei, M., Asare, R.A. & Tamakloe, B. (2010). *Leadership types/models*. Paper presented at Kongo University, Congo. Retrieved from http://www.slideshare.net/AmoahDaniel/leadership-types-5865434

Burns, J.M. (1978). *Leadership*. New York: Harper & Row.

Carlyle, T. (1907). *Heroes and hero worship*. Boston: Adams.

Case, C.M. (1933). Leadership and conjunction. *Sociology and Social Research*, 17, 510-513.

Cattell, R.B. (1951). New concepts for measuring leadership in terms of group syntality. *Human Relations*, 7, 161-184.

Dowd, J. (1936). *Control in human societies*. New York: Appleton-Century.

Evans, M.G. (1970). The effects of supervisory behavior on the path-goal relationship. *Organizational Behavior and Human Performance*, 5, 277- 298.

Fiedler, F.E. (1967). *A theory of leadership effectiveness*. New York: McGraw Hill.

Fleishman, E.A. (1953). The description of supervisory behavior. *Journal of Applied Psychology*, 37(1), 1-6.

Fleishman, E.A., Mumford, M.D., Zaccaro, S.J., Levin, K.Y., Korotkin, A.L. & Hein, M.B. (1991). Taxonomic efforts in the description of leader behavior: A synthesis and functional interpretation. *Leadership Quarterly*, 2(4), 245-287.

Galton, F. (1870). *Hereditary genius*. New York: Appleton.

Gerth, H. & Mills, C.W. (1953). Character *and social structure*. New York: Harcourt Brace.

Gray, E. & Smeltzer, L. (1989). *Management: The competitive edge*. New York: Macmillan.

Hackman, J.R. & Wageman, R. (2005). A Theory of Team Coaching. *Academy of Management Review*, 30(2), 269-287.

Hackman, J.R. & Walton, R.E. (1986). Leading groups in organizations. In P.S. Goodman (Ed.), *Designing effective work groups* (pp. 72–119). San Francisco: Jossey-Bass.

Heery, M. (1998). Winning Resources. *Library Management*, 19(4), 252-262.

Hemphill, J.K. (1955). Leadership behavior associated with the administrative reputations of college departments. *Journal of Educational Psychology*, 46, 385-401.

Hersey, P. & Blanchard, K.H. (1977). *Management of organizational behavior: Utilizing human resources*. Englewood Cliffs: Prentice-Hall.

Hocking, W.E. (1924). Leaders and led. *Yale Review*, 13, 625-641.

Homans, G.C. (1950). *The human group*. New York:Harcourt Brace.

Ingen, S.V. (2007). Leadership of Project Teams. *Chemical Engineering,* 114(1), 55-58.

Levine, M.F. (2000). *The importance of leadership: an investigation of presidential style at fifty national universities*. Paper presented at University of North Texas, USA. Retrieved from http://digital.library.unt.edu/ark:/67531/metadc2628/

Lovell, R.J. (1993). Power and the Project Manager. *International Journal of Project Management,* 11(2), 73-78.

McGrath, J.E. (1962). *Leadership behavior: Some requirements for leadership training*. Washington, D.C.: Civil Service Commission.

Mumford, E. (1909). *The origins of leadership*. Chicago: University of Chicago Press.

Stogdill, R.M. & Shartle, C.L. (1955). Methods *in the study of administrative leadership*. Columbus: Ohio State University.

Stogdill, R.M. (1948). Personal factors associated with leadership: a survey of the literature. *Journal of Psychology*, 25, 35-71.

Tead, O. (1935). *The art of leadership*. York, PA: McGraw-Hill.

Thompson, L.L. (2001). *The Mind and the Heart of the Negotiator*. New Jersey, USA: Prentice Hall.

Westburgh, E.M. (1931). A point of view: studies in leadership. *Journal of Abnormal and Social Psychology*, 25, 418-423.

Wiggam, A.E. (1931). *The biology of leadership*. New York: Pitman.

Woods, F.A. (1913). *The influence of monarchs*. New York: Macmillan.

Yu, L.H. (2006). *The Role of Leadership in Delivering A Successful Project*. Paper presented at University of Cambridge, UK. Retrieved from http://www.idbe.org/uploads/Li%20E1%20-%20IDBE12%20-%20The%20role%20of%20leadership%20in%20delivering%20a%20successful%20project.pdf

Zaccaro, S.J. (2007). Trait-based perspective. *American Psychology*, 62 (1), 7-16.

Zaccaro, S.J., Rittman, A.L. & Marks, M.A. (2001). Team leadership. *Leadership Quarterly*, 12(4), 451-483.